Natalie,

The Wonderful World
of
Madge Gill

Written and illustrated by Ayshea Ahmed

I hope you will enjoy this book!
Lots of love, Ayshea x

For Madge.

Based on a true story.

Introduction

Back in February 2011, I visited the Whitworth Art Gallery, as I often do, in my hometown of Manchester. An exhibition was being held there, entitled 'Intuition'.

It was on that day that one of the artists whose work was on display, whom I had not heard of before, grabbed me and pulled me into her world and that is where this story begins...

So many of the works on display were truly remarkable but there was something about a piece by Madge Gill that captured me immediately. I stood before it transfixed, trying to decipher what I was seeing.

On a long piece of calico cloth, around a metre long, I was confronted by a sea of faces appearing in a stream of consciousness; erratic, deep, inky black lines, at first nothing but a mass of marks, then in another moment they all made perfect, undulating sense.

There was no narrative, no beginning and no end. The work itself had a sense of infinity and one could easily imagine that it continued to exist beyond the confines of the physical page and that we were only glimpsing a small segment of something much more.

It certainly felt otherworldly, as if mystically imbued with a deep, radiative, feminine energy and a sense of the primary: the person, the artist, as well as the secondary, being the actual artwork itself.

I was immediately captivated and eager to know more about this person, her life and her work.

I was tantalised to discover that Madge claimed not to have created these works herself but rather that she was a vessel, a conduit for a spirit who had possessed her after she had seen a vision of Christ in the sky one day. She explained that this spirit channelled the work through her, guiding her hands, causing her to work for hours on end, sometimes in near darkness.

(photo courtesy of Edward Russell Westwood)

The name given to her spirit guide was Myrninerest, or 'My Inner Rest', and it was under this name that her works were signed. Despite receiving generous offers, Madge refused to sell any of these pieces, explaining that they were the not hers to sell as they were the property of Myrninerest. Upon her death in 1961, at the age of seventy-nine, hundreds of artworks were found intact within her home, stuffed into cupboards and drawers.

Her extraordinary life was as fascinating to me as her art and I decided to purchase a single, small original postcard of hers. I had it professionally framed and hung it on the wall in my living room. For nearly the next decade I went on to tell everyone who came to visit the story of Madge Gill.

I would look at the postcard with think, with admiration, about Madge's strength in the face of adversity, her abandonment issues as a child, her endurance in later life and the physical toll of creating the work itself, whilst dealing with a tragic and painful past.

She was an incredibly unique woman and she created the art that she wanted, disregarding what anyone thought of its, or her own, perceived eccentricities.

I always knew that I wanted to write a small, illustrated book about her, to honour her life and to share her story with everyone, young and old, and so this project began.

My aim was to give life to her story and create a background for her art with my illustrations. Images would come to mind of the vision of Christ and her possession, her sitting in bed all night drawing and the postcards stuffed into drawers. I started to sketch some of my ideas out and this book began to form and take shape.

(Photography by Lawrence Robinson GCF)

Like two other great women, Coco Chanel and Marilyn Monroe, Madge was orphaned as a child and left to make her way in the world alone. Similarly, she also managed to leave an indelible mark on the annals of artistic history reaching far beyond her life and her death.

During the writing of this book, sadly, my father passed away and work stopped for a while but as I picked up my pen again and started to draw, I became engrossed once more and realised that this has been my inner rest too.

I am so happy to share her story with you now.

I hope it will inspire you to always remember Madge Gill and her amazing art.

Best wishes to you all,

Ayshea

Madge Gill was born against the gloomy backdrop of Victorian London in Walthamstow, North East London, on the 19th of January 1882, under the astrological sign of Capricorn.

Her given name at birth was Maude Ethel Eades but later in life she came to be known simply as Madge Gill.

Madge went on to have a remarkable and in some parts tragic life but it was those dramatic events that would ultimately shape her as a person and contribute to the prolific and enigmatic output of work that she went on to produce during her lifetime.

Although she would not have been considered to be famous whilst she was alive, she is now deemed to be one of most intriguing and highly regarded Outsider Artists* of the twentieth century.

*The late, great Roger Cardinal originally coined the term 'Outsider Art' in 1972. Since then it has been taken to mean self-taught. Outsider artists did not pursue fame, money or success, worked in isolation and existed outside of the mainstream art world.

Madge as a little girl

Name: Maude Ethel Eades, later Madge Gill.

Born: 1882, London, Died 1961.

Places lived: England and Canada

Hobbies: Drawing, Painting, Sewing, knitting, Weaving, Writing, Singing, prophesising about the future.

Interests: Spiritualism, Astrology, Tarot cards, Clairvoyancy, looking after her children.

Unfortunately, after her birth, Madge's mother Emma Eades was unable to look after her daughter by herself.

Emma had been unmarried when Madge was born and this was considered to be shameful during the Victorian era, with its strict moral values and codes. Her child's illegitimacy also meant that Emma would not have been entitled to any financial assistance from the government to help to provide for her.

It was also rumoured that Emma may have suffered from learning difficulties or mental health challenges and these issues were among the reasons that she was unable to offer Madge the care that she would have required.

The sad decision was made to have Madge placed into foster care with another family, where she could be properly looked after. It was also a bid to keep her 'embarrassing' existence a secret.

Her grandfather originally paid the other family to look after Madge but when he could no longer keep up with the payments, a further decision was made to send her to an orphanage for destitute children called Dr Barnardo's. The year was 1891 and Madge was only nine years old when she was taken to the orphanage and left there all alone.

During this emotionally difficult time, one would hope that the young Madge found some solace in the classes provided, like bible studies, needlework, knitting and other domestic skills, which, given Madge's later creative passions, were likely of great influence.

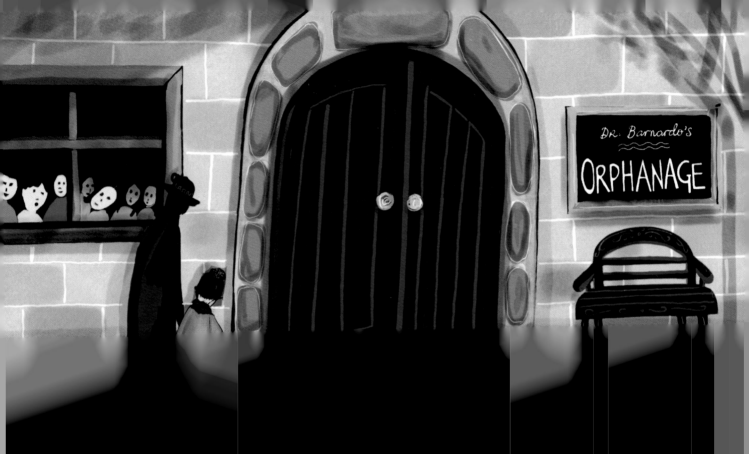

After staying at the orphanage for five years, Madge was sent to Canada in 1896 along with a large number of their other British orphans, as part of the 'Home Children's Scheme'. The scheme was a labour programme intended to offer poor and destitute children prospects and opportunities that they would not normally have had in England at that time. Although their intentions were good and the scheme seemed to make sense (to provide fresh air and the possibility of a better, healthier life for children from overcrowded and unhygienic London slums), many of the children on the scheme were miserable, unhappy and mistreated there.

With much resilience, Madge spent four hard, long years working as a servant on a string of farms in Ontario.

Her duties would have included babysitting, performing daily, household chores, or even doing manual labour on the land.

It was gruelling work with only meagre pay and Madge longed to return to England as an adult and to see her friends and family once again.

By the time she was eighteen, she had managed to save up enough money to buy herself a ticket back to the place that she called home.

It was on this journey home that 'Maude' decided to rename herself 'Madge' as if cutting ties to her old life and making entry into a new one.

After returning to England in 1900 she tried to forget about her time in Canada.

And life was to change for her yet again…

Happy to be back, Madge found herself work as a nurse at Whipps Cross Hospital in Leytonstone and things started to look up at last.

She also became reacquainted with her Aunt Kate, who was, by all accounts, an extremely interesting woman, often conducting seances to contact the spirits of the dead, reading Tarot cards and drawing up astrological charts.

It was Kate who introduced Madge to the world of the supernatural, which included Astrology, Mediumship, Clairvoyance and Cheiromancy. All popular topics in the Victorian and Edwardian eras, Madge took an intense interest in these and other esoteric subjects.

Madge went on to set herself up as a practising medium and was known to prophesise about other people's futures. (Some of her predictions actually came true according to letters written about her after her death).

It was here, at Kate's home, that Madge grew closer to Kate's son (and thus her cousin), Tom Gill, whom she later went on to marry.

ASTROLOGY

It was in 1907, in Chelsea where they were now living, that Tom and Madge were legally married at the local Town Hall. They later moved to Pelham Road, South Woodford, and were blessed with three beautiful sons: Laurie, Reggie and Bob.

But sadly, the happiness was not to last.

Madge and Tom get married

Home Sweet Home

They have three sons:
Laurie, Reggie & Bob.

Tom and Madge were heartbroken when at only eight years of age their beloved second son Reggie died during the influenza pandemic of 1918.

Then tragedy struck once more, only a year later, when Madge gave birth again, this time, sadly, to a stillborn baby girl.

As if things weren't bad enough, during that time, Madge herself came close to death and was confined to her bed for several months.

Sadly, one of the results of her illness was the loss of one of her eyes, which had to be removed and replaced with a false one made of glass.

Things can't have been easy for Madge. Tom was away fighting in World War Two and she was struggling, dealing with grief, health problems and looking after her remaining children, but again, she endured it all and found the strength to carry on for herself and for her family.

One day in 1920, after her recovery from her eye operation, Madge was in high spirits, doing the housework and singing the song 'Home Sweet Home' at the top of her lungs. She was singing so loudly in fact that she could heard throughout the length of the street.

She went outside into the garden with her two sons and looked up into the sky.

There, she was greeted by an incredible vision of a crucified Jesus, floating on a cross, accompanied by angels. Madge proclaimed that she had looked into another world and she had seen crowds and the faces of people including Dr Barnardo himself and a great number of children.

It was this sight in the sky that was the catalyst for her sudden, passionate and obsessive interest in drawing, sewing, knitting, singing and writing, all of which she began in earnest.

From that point onwards Madge explained that she had been possessed by a spirit who flowed through her hands to create these artworks.

It was for this reason that Madge refused to sell any of her work as she believed that they were not her own creations but rather the property of a friendly but nebulous spirit whom she referred to as 'Myrninerest'. It was always under this name that she signed her work. Many have speculated that this name was Madge's own secret language for 'My Inner Rest'.

We cannot know for sure whether Madge was authentically channelling Myrninerest but it is what she believed to be true and this connection was certainly a factor and the driving force behind her creative output.

Her possession by Myrninerest would remain for nearly the rest of her life and together they created thousands of magical drawings, paintings, embroideries, knitted pieces and automatic writings.

With only the use of one eye, Madge worked obsessively on her intricate designs with incredible precision, often working throughout the night in near darkness.

Without a studio she would work wherever she could.

Madge's drawings primarily featured the same subject, female faces and forms, appearing over and over and over again, fading in and out and often wearing fantastical outfits, with incredible hats and expressions.

These beautiful and extraordinary women seem eternally enmeshed within a gossamer fabric of geometric architectural webs, complex networks of lines and crosses, chessboards, staircases, crosshatched, tessellating patterns and designs whilst also incorporating some of the organic designs of nature. There is almost a kinetic energy to many of her pieces, they look like they are flowing and moving and your eyes follow the lines.

Who knows if those mysterious girls represent Madge herself, or the daughter she lost?

Was it the vision in the sky with the crowds of people? Could the faces portray the different stages or facets of Madge's life or her personality or do they represent the face of Myrninerest? It is certainly part of the mystique of Madge's story.

Some people speculated that the faces were those of the dead souls of the previous occupants of the house in which she now lived, killed by bombs during the war.

When questioned, Madge refused to disclose the identity of the figures but she did say that each face had its own significance for her and this is certainly something to ponder.

Madge's drawings always featured the face

of a girl appearing again and again.

Madge also worked tirelessly on huge textile pieces, knitting, weaving and sewing with vividly coloured threads.

She often wore frocks constructed from these brightly coloured fabrics, feeling that the wearing of the dress next to her skin would keep her closer to Myrninerest.

Many of these garments and tapestries survive and now belong in renowned art collections around the world.

Driven by the unseen hands of Myrninerest, Madge also produced a huge amount of automatic writings in pen and ink, mainly working on paper and card.

The writings consisted of words, shapes, letters, hieroglyphs and mystic symbols and were all scribed in a beautiful calligraphic script.

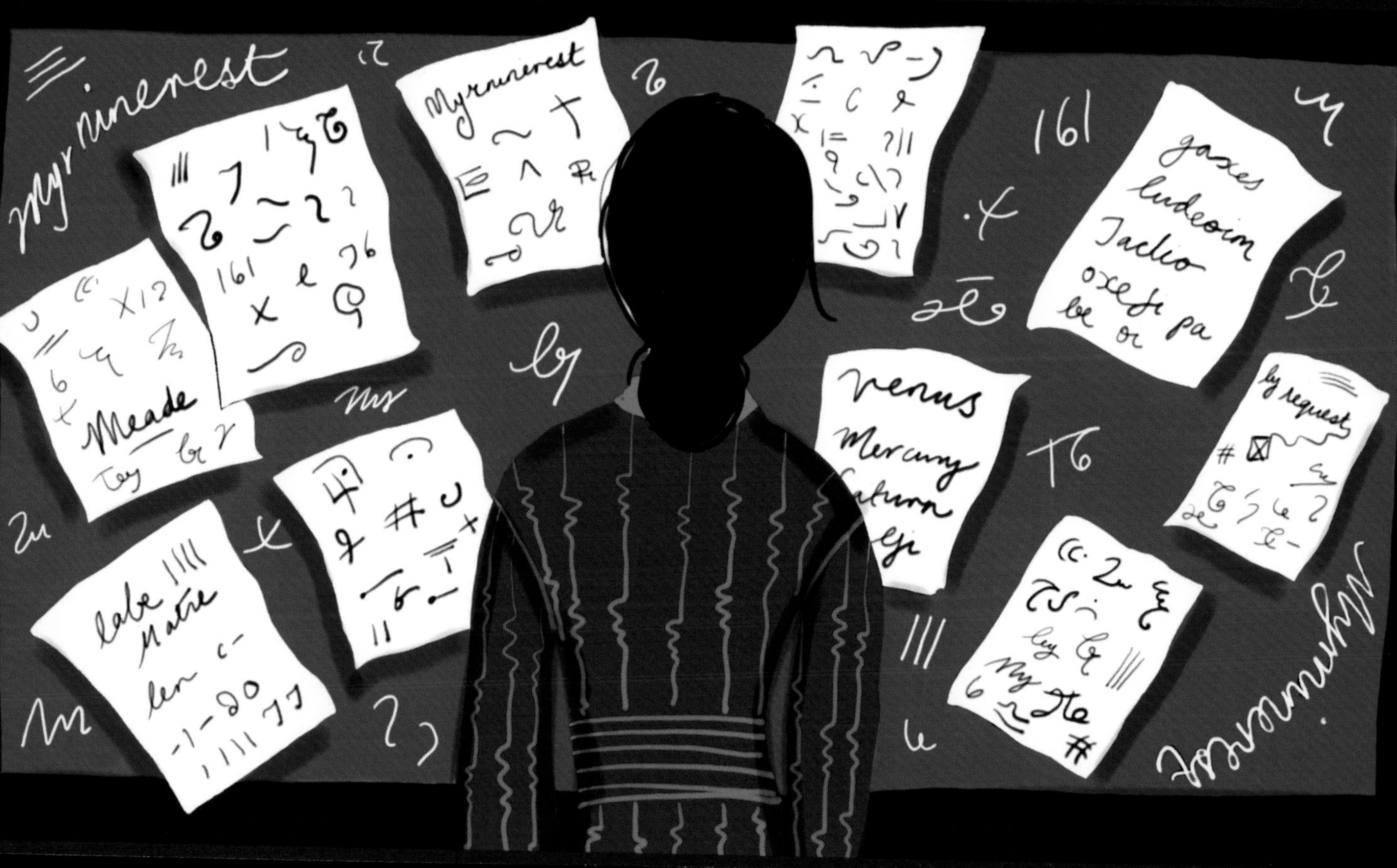

Venus
Mercury
Meade
by request
gases
161

Her compulsion to work was relentless. The size of her works ranged from postcard size to works on calico that were tens of metres long. Madge referred to the calico as 'Balloon Cloth' and explained that she had bought these huge swathes of fabric in a sale of surplus fabric left over from World War One.

She would work on one single length of this cloth unravelled on a roller (reminiscent of a Japanese scroll), just enough to draw on it section by section. This enabled her to work in a stream of consciousness and without interruption. Some of the works were too large to display or even look at inside the house and often she could not see the start of the drawing by the time she came to the end.

Word got out about Madge's incredible artworks and in 1945 a charming photographer called Edward visited her at home and took several fabulous photographs of her at work. Madge's son Laurie helped her to hang a gigantic, completed calico out along the walls of the garden so that it could be viewed in all its glorious entirety.

People really started to notice Madge's work, often mesmerised by the intricate and hypnotic swirling patterns and faces. The story of her possession by Myrninerest made people even more intrigued. These were some of the reasons why her work was included in many exhibitions, most regularly at The Whitechapel Gallery in London.

Again, Madge refused to sell any of the works as she did not want to displease Myrninerest, under whose influence she went on to create thousands of these ethereal, spiritual artworks over the ensuing forty years, stopping only briefly during the last years of her life.

19ᵗʰ Aug
1947

Madge Gill died aged seventy-nine on the 28th January 1961 at Langhorne Hospital in Leytonstone, not far from where she had lived for over twenty years at 37 Plashet Grove, Upton Park.

Madge outlived two of her sons; Reggie died in 1918 and her youngest son Bob died in 1950. She also outlived her husband Tom, who died in 1933.

After her death, her only surviving son Laurie gathered hundreds of pieces of Madge's work which were stored around the house, stuffed into drawers and cupboards and under the bed.

He donated the majority of the works to East Ham Council where they were looked after very carefully by a kind man called James Green, who went on to hold an exhibition in Madge's honour in 1969. Some of her other artworks were sold and some of the larger pieces (measuring many metres) were possibly destroyed as they may have been too difficult to store or exhibit. Others of her works were sold to private individuals at auction and often taken to other countries.

For years after her death, Madge's work remained largely forgotten by the wider public but in 2019 an exhibition was held at the prestigious William Morris Gallery in Walthamstow, igniting an interest in her again, as thousands of people came to marvel at her phenomenal and dazzling art.

Madge Gill
ink on
Calico

Madge never intended or sought to be famous and never attended any formal art lessons. Her artistic gifts were truly innate.

We cannot know for sure whether Madge was compelled to do the work either for her own inner rest, or if it was all at the behest of Myrninerest, and so the enigma remains.

Madge Gill
1882 — 1961

In the years following Madge's death, her works found their way into in several public art collections, including the Aracine Collection in Lille, France and the Collection de l'Art Brut in Lausanne, Switzerland, appearing in many exhibitions.

In 2010, the Trustees of the Musgrave Kinley Outsider Art Collection generously donated a large collection of Outsider Art to the Whitworth Art Gallery in Manchester, where Madge's pieces are now often displayed.

In 2018, Waltham Forest Council put up a prestigious Blue Plaque in her honour on the wall of the flat where she was born at 71 High Street, Walthamstow.

Then in 2019, a large mural was painted in tribute to her onto the side of a local building, featuring Madge as the star.

So now, Madge Gill will never be forgotten and her work and legacy continues to inspire others to this day.

Credits, references, further reading and notes:

Most of my illustrations are based on the incredible photographs taken by Edward Russell Westwood of Madge and Laurie at her home in Plashet, East Ham on August 19th, 1947.

Credits:

I could not have written this book without constant reference to the brilliant website http://madgegill.com/ which was created through the meticulous work of a lovely lady called Vivienne Roberts.

Her amazing website covers Madge's life in much detail, including a biography and chronology of her life, images of her artworks, and a list of past and future exhibitions and events.

Vivienne also has another website called mediumisticart.com which is a great resource if you are interested in looking at other channelled artworks.

Another invaluable source when writing this was the book Madge Gill by Myrninerest which is edited by Sophie Dutton and published by Rough Trade Books. It includes lots of reference material, photographs, anecdotal stories and letters. Sophie also curated the wonderful Madge Gill exhibition at the William Morris Gallery in 2019.

There is also a fascinating interview available online entitled My Love to You Who Knows where Sophie has a very interesting chat with a lovely man called Michael Morgan Theis who knew Madge as a child and watched her working on her drawings during his youth, which he describes in much detail.

The first written piece that I ever read about Madge was the Intuition Exhibition booklet from the Whitworth Gallery in Manchester, where an exhibition of the same name was held in 2011, after the donation of the Musgrove Kinley collection to the gallery in 2010.

There is a great video called Madge Gill Discussion on YouTube on the Orleans House Gallery channel where Madge's life is discussed.

Raw Vision Magazine is a wonderful magazine for anyone interested in knowing more about Outsider Art. I used issue 87 for reference which has Madge as the cover girl and there is a fascinating article inside by a nice lady called Sara Ayad.

The Henry Boxer Gallery specialises in Outsider Art and the website is a great way to look at and learn more about the works of many amazing Outsider Artists, including Madge Gill. The gallery website is https://www.outsiderart.co.uk/

The commemorative mural at Madge Gill's birthplace was created through the partnership of Works by Madge Gill and Wood Street Walls and the owners of the wall, Lazer Group. The mural was beautifully designed by Paddy Molly and painted by a fantastic artist called PANG.

Other sources used:

https://voicesofspirit.wordpress.com/2013/10/10/madge-gill-medium-visionary/

https://www.raggedschoolmuseum.org.uk/2015/11/23/ragged-children-mended-lives/

https://wrldrels.org/2018/03/07/madge-gill/DanielWojcik

https://en.wikipedia.org/wiki/Madge_Gill

Star of Destiny; Madge Gill and Spiritualism, by Vivienne Roberts -an essay from Madge Gill by Myrninerest, edited by Sophie Dutton.

Borderlands – Dr Boyle and the Genesis of Gill's Art by Sara Ayad - an essay from Madge Gill by Myrninerest, edited by Sophie Dutton.

Madge Gill and the Art Brut Collection in Lausanne by Sarah Lombardi - an essay from Madge Gill by Myrninerest, edited by Sophie Dutton.

Raw Vision Magazine – Issue 87 Article by Sara Ayad 'The Arts and Crafts of Madge Gill' you can still order a copy of this Madge Gill edition from https://rawvision.com/

Bastardy and Baby Farming in Victorian England

by Dorothy L. Haller http://people.loyno.edu/~history/journal/1989-0/haller.htm
(This paper was selected by the Department of History as the Outstanding Paper for the 1989-1990 academic year).

https://en.wikipedia.org/wiki/Madge_Gill

https://spitalfieldslife.com/2018/12/16/looking-for-madge-gill/

https://rawvision.com/artist/madge-gill

https://www.messynessychic.com/2020/01/28/meet-mrs-madge-gill-the-outsider-artist-who-painted-through-the-spirit-world/

http://press.woodstreetwalls.co.uk/167116-public-asked-to-select-choose-the-design-of-new-mural-of-celebrated-outsider-artist-madge-gill

https://woodstreetwalls.typeform.com/to/fQ6oE3

https://accessalliance.co.uk/2019/01/30/star-platforms-help-bring-the-madge-gill-mural-to-life/

Images of original Madge Gill artworks were kindly supplied Courtesy Newham Archives Local Studies Library. A special thank you to Jenni Munro-Collins.

Artists who have directly or indirectly inspired my illustrations:

Madge Gill, David Hockney, early Andy Warhol, Gauguin , Evelyn Dunbar, Quentin Blake, Van Gogh, Cezanne, Matisse, Henri Rousseau, Monet, Picasso, Eric Gill, Nasreen Mohamedi, Celia Birtwell, Barbara Hulanicki, Francis Bacon, Clare Leighton, Jackson Pollock, George Le Pape, Joan Eardley, Constable, Rembrandt (the washing in the basket is inspired by his turban), Camille Bombois, Degas, Vivian Maier, Aubrey Beardsley, William Morris, Eric Ravillious, Ellen Dryden, Saira Ahmed, Paula Hillis, Robert Haigh-McLane.

I would like to thank the following people for their love and support during the writing of this book.

Enis Muminovic, Nadim Dar, Kausar Dar, Saira Ahmed, Tahira Dar, Shehla Dar, Sean Cowlishaw, Yasmin Patel, Laura McNamara, Marie Masson, Anne Malone, Andrew McKendry, Angela Gilmartin, Fiona Cartledge, Violet Bradley, Super Dacob, Iestyn Williams, Francis B, Vivian M, Madge Gill.

Finally, a massive thank you to Kirsty-Ellen Smillie and the team at Cranthorpe Millner Publishers for their guidance and support.

In Loving Memory of Mohammed Nadim Dar.

1941-2020

About the author.

Ayshea Ahmed was born in 1973 in Manchester, England, under the astrological sign of Scorpio.

After studying Fashion at the University of Derby she moved to London, working at Sign of the Times in Covent Garden and Hyper Hyper on Kensington High Street, before returning to Manchester and beginning a corporate career in Sales lasting for twenty years.

Ayshea decided to leave her job in 2020 to pursue her passion for painting, drawing and writing.

The Wonderful World of Madge Gill is her first book and she plans to write about other lesser known artists and bring their stories to life through her simple narrative and expressive illustrations.

You can view some of her original artworks on Instagram: AysheaArt and on Facebook: Ayshea Ahmed, Artist.
Instagram - @madgegillbook

Photography by Laura McNamara.
Ceramics by Katch Skinner and Bridie Hall.
Paintings by Ayshea Ahmed.
Vogue Mirror - Illustration is by Ellen Dryden.
Madge Gill postcard in the background.